Poverty Creek Anthology:

An Appalachian Memoir in Haiku

Poverty Creek Anthology:
An Appalachian Memoir in Haiku

Nancy Bagato

Stilt Leg Press
2017

First Printing: 2017

ISBN 978-0-998-5981-1-6

Stilt Leg Press
26 Kerr Street
Onancock, Virginia 23417

U.S> trade bookstores and wholesalers: Please contact
Stilt Leg Press. Tel. (540) 314-9512 or e-mail enbee1@hotmail.com

Contents

Introduction 3

Summer 4

Autumn...48

Winter 85

Spring..112

Introduction

a kaleidoscope
of small tragedies and
small miracles: nature.

Summer

July first.
cicada rattle.
it's summer.

earthworm, hot asphalt.
each end gropes in opposite
directions, feebly.

highway median.
off-season turkey watches
hunters pass slowly.

thin old man, bare,
red as rusted nail, droops
fishing line into traffic.

jelly egg body,
tiny T-rex arms for legs.
tadpole swims idly.

moonlight. girl staggers.
her cigarette falls into
serenade guitar.

heads low and locked,
circling slowly,
bovine tango.

"What Would Jesus Build"
graffiti tattoo on wood
at construction site.

jackpot! shiny black truck,
black garbage bags inside.
big black crow chows down.

huge ripe tomatoes

on old man's porch, welcome bribe

for conversation.

breathe in tangy smell
of toddler sweat, storm cloud hair,
her favorite shoes.

child barefoot in hot sun.
cold, sweet watermelon, juice
dripping down chin, arms.

Chinese melon vines,
lovingly tended. landlord
uprooted as weeds.

candy smokes, sold out.
a lottery ticket, with no
penny to scratch.

young Black man, arm 'round
bleached blonde, watches laundromat
TV. no laundry.

clockwork: 5 p.m.
cloud of pigeons bursts from roof,
circles and returns.

porcine bank tellers
cross street heavy unsteady
on white cloven feet.

satin evening gowns,
red, white, blue. grand opening girls
glide into store.

small head, big truck.

ears, halved butterflies spread wide.

plate, bicentennial.

roadside bounty of
misspelled fruit. caramel wood
weights syrupy air.

boy in overalls.
bantam pullet sleeps on knee.
rural flea market.

state fair. young hunchback
in cowboy hat smiles shyly
over soda pop.

hands push hard on back.

needle cuts skin: blood and ink.

he sings as he works.

heat lightning, headlights.

cigarettes, speaker, popcorn.

movie in the trees.

constellation of
treetop fireflies: flickering,
passionate dying.

angus herd,
black as oil slick, stains
tree shadow.

choking smell. goat skull
in creek, no horns. hole between eyes.
loose hair on bank.

squirrel, belly-up.

white ribs, spine gleam through leather.

permanent x-ray.

red cardinal bends
over flattened mate until next
car rushes over.

gliding across grass,
black cat, shadow with eye holes
showing lawn behind.

fat green June beetles
whirr in heavy low circles
over white clover.

heavy-headed sway.

peonies seduce ants with

sticky sweet pinkness.

last black wasp hovers over
crushed paper and bodies. freeze—
guilt smeared on my boots.

big hands, tail tip white.
fleshy nose (tiny finger)
sniffs at me. mole digs.

grasshopper eyes peer
over kitchen curtain, jerk
behind when spotted.

marching river edge,

claws held high, huge green crawdad,

sand on all eight feet.

shrew in blood puddle,
seedy grass stem clenched in teeth
like a tango rose.

red-eyed cicadas
by the hundreds hatch, call, mate,
die in mid-flight.

striped spider,
web in grass: zipper
half-unzipped.

roadside breakdown.

heat, no wind. hummingbird buzzed,

pipping as it passed.

cheap shoes. through
blisters, feet become
rotten fruit.

loneliest mailbox.

perfect web, a waiting spider,

fill open doorway.

seeds float on
late summer breeze
like daughter's giggles.

Autumn

at my heels, breeze
lifts leaves in sudden spiral.
i walk creating fall.

overgrown alley:
boozy smell of fallen fruit
rotting underfoot.

young Black trucker
plays sweet sockhop songs
on diner jukebox.

Pontiac muscle.

hood chicken. antique plates,

younger than me.

small brown child waits

for turtle, held like a fat

sandwich, to emerge.

starlings peer from roof holes,

gutters gone. below, thin

cats cringe under cars.

earthworm snake, black up,
pink down, coils between fingers.
living jewelry.

tiny rat in rain
peering into shop windows
like Oliver Twist.

four months of dampness.
basement sprouts forest of
delicate frilled ears.

two robin thrushes,

wings folded neatly, feet curled,

breasts rusting in sun.

from birthing

themselves, mountains

worn and yellow.

distant ringing phone
tickles me out of light sleep:
woodpecker dials up bugs.

seagulls shriek
in cornfield stubble.
strange harvest.

hundreds of tiny
brown mushrooms on oak tree roots:
freckles on redhead.

thorny twig tangle.
cardinal plucks rosehip.
guarded heart stolen.

electric mousetrap.

two tiny mice balled inside

like peas in a pod.

trap fails. released mouse

scrambles, foot twisted behind.

cruelty or kindness?

dollar coins scattered
by rain, car-crushed. old-man mouths.
small snappers, fight gone.

young bulls bunch up in
the dark road, wild and lonesome
as Johnny Cash songs.

moon, fog, field. horses drift.

ghost shadows, muffled hooves.

dark premonitions.

between apartments
and road, statue in small creek
strikes: night heron eats.

blown leaf: small torn bat
creeps down hall, dust, hair tangled
around leaf-stem bones.

muddy turtle drags
withered mummy leg behind,
flat bone, thin bone bare.

hind leg peeled and crushed,

prone rabbit watches me.

both of us still, helpless.

deep in raw thorn bush,
deer skull, spine trailing to earth.
chewed green antlers.

small pale millipedes,

spirals in shrew flesh decay.

predator and prey.

pink clouds sleeping low.
dark masked horses moving slow.
cotton candy dawn.

dead-end road. crushed crawdads,
green huge dozen, claws open,
halfway back to creek.

glistening spiral
slug trail, architect dead at
labyrinth center.

empty house, tall weeds.
two cats twine tails together
like honeymooners.

drought. fierce thunderstorm
brings tiny toads—red, gold, brown.
jewels on fall leaves.

on brown leaf, two slugs
curl amorously, circle
gleaming mucous pearl.

storm-soaked basement. quick!
a wiggle under wet cardboard:
gold salamander.

cleaning flowerbed
(nails, rocks, dead bulbs), small snake
slithers between hands.

deer lift one by one,
effortless, sweet as breeze.
white salute over wire.

early morning sun:

flat white disk in dense white sky.

illusion in fog.

Winter

this one year, i am
minding the kudzu, how it burns
with the first frost.

pumpkin-head snowman:
stick arms embrace long autumn
and sudden winter.

squirrel perches on wire,
dark comma on lined paper
of white winter sky.

dead (frozen?)
crawdad stirs in hand.
milagro.

dirty white horses
on brown hill, posed and still as
unpainted concrete.

November. twilight road.
trucker's obscene gesture
with knackwurst fingers.

beige and gray trailers,
sediment deposited
at mountain bottom.

tin roof rain music
in milky plastic cocoon:
trailer park winter.

brick wall, pipes leading
nowhere. cardboard-patched window.
gray sky wind swings wires.

Poff's Motor Palace:

shipwrecked car hulls, old tractors,

gravel and ghost town.

see red. on closed door,
bruise knuckle where "e" of "love"
or "hate" would be tattooed.

two starlings wrestle
foot in beak, wings spread flutter.
seraphim in dirt.

mid-winter
cold snap. geese fly
farther south.

all-day hunt,
no luck. evening falls,
deer graze yard.

crazy man in bar
Christmas eve, alone with his
angels and devils.

white glitter
swirling, never lands:
snowglobe world.

puddles freeze
into ocean waves
from cold wind.

branches crushed, curbside
evergreen waits for trash truck.
tinsel flutters, shines.

porch roof sags, shingles gone.

sugar windows broken.

January gingerbread house.

bright hearts tossed in snow
mutter "hey baby, hot stuff."
candy harassment.

premature
robins listen for
frozen worms.

loud rustling,
rain of red berries.
waxwing swarm.

smart mouse, caught at last.

released far from house, looks back

for a long moment.

mockingbird
copies mutt whining
on tie rope.

too many feathers,
not enough bird. long shadows bring
rooster strutting home.

thin grass blades,
green and ochre through snow.
beard stubble.

Spring

after long winter
without insects, moth diving
to its death startles.

light bursts into life.
golden mercury floats, falls.
gray day goldfinches.

thin boy leans into
strong wind. thunderous crinkling
of plastic bag kite.

quiet man
smiles softly, bare arms
wet with rain.

smoky clouds
glide down mountainsides,
soft fingers.

trace constellations

on his body, freckle to mole,

from mole to scar.

cherry blossoms fall
piece by piece: lips, fingertips,
breasts, pink on pavement.

Mexican workers
balanced on steel skeleton
sing to girls below.

small snakes mate twisted

on flotsam. large snake rests,

skin ripped over pink flesh.

mud-brown larvae split,
extrude themselves. crumpled wings.
harden green in sun.

day-old chicks
hungrily pull on
own pink worm toes.

hummingbird stillness.
loose feather jewels float, catch
gently on snapbeans.

crow fledgling sprawled, legs
impossibly long, skull crushed.
dead mother nearby.

broad black thundercloud sow,

raindrop piglets jostling round,

sudden as spring rain.

muddaub barn swallows
shriek above mummified hide.
green clouds fill silo.

exploded toad

coughed broken bones

onto road.

teardrop koi, startling red

in brown water, reflect

start of miscarriage.

black beast (wide white teeth)
on small black road, charged my car
and melted—a ghost.

horned legs downside up,
fat bright night caterpillar
rolls, strolls on moonlight.

month-old squirrel sleeps
in my hat, thin tail curled round
her crumpled brown ears.

baby in shoebox:

possum feeds self peaches,

spoon held in monkey foot.

teenagers poke heads
out of car, freakshow turtle
basking in spring sun.

henhouse rooster crows.
yard rooster crows. man in house
yawns out Tarzan yell.

urban camouflage:
Hawaiian shirt bleeds into
ink of tattooed arms.

small boy, bad haircut.

stray hairs stick out behind ears.

down on baby bird.

robin flap and jerk,
yanking, stretching worm long, short, long.
cartoon bird.

dirigible cat
bulges her unborn kittens
towards my hand.

www.ingramcontent.com/pod-product-compliance
Lightning Source LLC
Chambersburg PA
CBHW030019290326
41934CB00005B/410